DIASPORA CAFÉ: D.C.

EDITED BY JEFFREY BANKS AND MARITZA RIVERA

Diaspora Café: D.C. © Day Eight, 2022

Each poem individually © the author, printed by permission

Cover art © Sami Miranda and Lazaro Batista, used by permission

Book design by Shannon Pallatta

About the Editors

JEFFREY BANKS is poetically known as "Big Homey." His credits include: ESSENCE Magazine, Sirius/XM Satellite Radio, Radio-One Inc., the CBS Early Show, BLACKENTERPRISE Magazine, performing nationwide, international broadcasts, multiple grant awards and publications through DC Public Libraries, the National Association forPoetry Therapy, Paris Lit Up, and Day Eight.

MARITZA RIVERA is a Puerto Rican poet and Army veteran who has lived in Rockville, MD since 1994. She has been writing poetry for over fifty years; is the creator of a short form of poetry called Blackjack and is the publisher of Casa Mariposa Press. In 2011, Maritza began hosting the annual Mariposa Poetry Retreat, "where the magic of poetry happens", which takes place in Puerto Rico in 2022. Maritza is the author of About You; A Mother's War, written during her son's two tours in Iraq; Baker's Dozen; Twenty-One: Blackjack Poems and creator of the Blackjack Poetry Playing Cards. Her work appears in literary magazines, anthologies andonline publications and in the public arts project, Meet Me at the Triangle in Wheaton, MD.

Early Response To Diaspora Café DC

The voices brought together by Banks and Rivera in this important book represent a rich range of poetry of witness across the diaspora. They are fierce voices, brazenly claiming their histories, full of love and beauty and gracefully defiant. Voices that, as Jane Alberdeston Coralin puts it in *Transient*, are still "...migrating, always coming / and going, from one island to another, / from factory floor to pavement, from wharf to plank / to whipping seas." Such poems as Nick Leininger's *The First Time I Felt Black* invite us to consider the spectrum of lived experience and remind us, as Hermond Palmer does in *I am Joaquin*, that "Your history / is my history / Your future / my future."

—Naomi Ayala, author of *Wild Animals on the Moon and Other Poems*, *This Side of Early*, and *Calling Home: Praise Songs and Incantations*

Diaspora Cafe is a soaring collection full of the power, pain, joy and blood of vibrant voices. These voices stir and sing; they'll shake you to your roots. Henry Reneau Jr. in "El Dia de Los Muertos" says, "We are not a footnote. Are not a trend" and indeed the poems in this book demand to be read. This is an incredible, necessary collection.

—Jennifer Maritza McCauley, author of *SCAR ON/SCAR OFF* and *When Trying to Return Home*

What a glorious, animated, convivial, compendium Jeffrey Banks and Maritza Rivera have edited. Here are 14 of your favorite poets with words that fly off the page with originality and truth. Uplifting and colorful, this is Salsa, Bachata, and Cha Cha. This is energy in language.

—Grace Cavalieri, Maryland Poet Laureate

"A moving collection of poems—Diaspora Cafe is an honest and tender portrayal of the complexities we experience while thriving and surviving within the African diaspora."

—Danyeli Rodriguez Del Orbe, author of *Periodicos De Ayer*

"If I lived near the Diaspora Café, I'd post up here for coffee every morning. We need to read lines like "If we treated every child like poetry" and "Neruda's head is across town" and "The first time I felt black" and "Your body is my favorite chocolate" and "Nothing seemed more important / than chips with ketchup" and "God, whose father was a cane / cutter." The poems Jeffrey Banks and Maritza Rivera gather here are voice and burn, kiss and blade, stranger and friend. These poems give us a place to stay when we are far from home, which is all the time."

—Joseph Ross, author of *Raising King and Ache*

"The poems in "Diaspora Café" take readers on a journey into Afro-Latinidad that ventures beyond skin color, one's last name, or the Spanish language. This book is a mirror of the past that also reflects the present and the future of the complex and beautiful mosaic that is Afro Latino culture in the Washington area and in the USA."

—Alberto Roblest, author of *Against the Wall*

"Los poemas de "Diáspora Café" llevan a los lectores en un viaje por la afrolatinidad que va más allá del color de la piel, el apellido o el idioma español. Este libro es un espejo del pasado que también refleja el presente y el futuro del complejo y hermoso mosaico que es la cultura afrolatina en el área de Washington y en los Estados Unidos."

—Alberto Roblest, author of *Against the Wall*

"Diaspora Cafe is a rich dialogue across cultures; sharing stories that do the important work of recognizing both difference and similarities. This collection not only sees culture and color but celebrates it through the universal language of poetry."

—Dwayne Lawson-Brown, author of *One Color Kaleidoscope* and *Twenty:21*

Editor's Note from Jeffrey Banks

I'm honored to serve as the initiator of the Diaspora Café project, as well as the co-editor of this book. I selected the word "Diaspora" to describe the African diaspora, including the diversity of Black ethnic culture globally on all the continents and the Caribbean. "Café" is a Spanish word for "brown" as well as a word associated with poetry venues. People of LatinX heritage embody many shades of a "brown" as our diversity ranges from European Spaniards, to native peoples in Latin American communities, to the undeniable African ancestry of LatinX populations whose descendants have darker skin than many Black Americans (but may be insulted if someone thinks of them as "Negro", a Spanish word for "Black".)

Without calling out any specific population, it always baffled me growing up how different classmates similar or darker than my skin color didn't consider themselves "Black" even knowing that in any civil rights or police issue that is how they would be identified. The acronym for Diaspora Café is "D.C.", letters synonymous to the District of Columbia. This opportunity was created to celebrate a talented group of writers poetically articulating the Black and Brown experience in America from the D.C. region. Thanks to my co-editor, Maritza Rivera, a Nubian Queen from Puerto Rico, including for translating some of the works in this collection. Thanks also to Robert Bettmann and Day Eight who graciously worked with me to overcome several hurdles in creating this project.

This literary collection features ethnic populations often misunderstood. I'm grateful to all of the poets sharing their work so African-American and LatinX cultures can have a better understanding of each other (and all readers can have a better understanding of us!) There are stereotypes communities of color hold on to that fester prejudicial views and ethnic infighting. Black and LatinX neighborhoods/barrios work better together instead of being adversaries. My hope is to grow this project to further spread this message.

To God be the Glory/a Dios sea la Gloria! Blacks & LatinX Matter (BLM)! Live/Viva

Editor's Note from Maritza Rivera

I want to first thank Jeffrey Banks for inviting me to join him as co-editor of the AfroLatinX Anthology. This has been a tremendous opportunity for me to continue discovering the magic of poetry.

My poetry journey began at an early age when I discovered the power and magic of words. Poetry helped me paint pictures that I could otherwise not articulate. To me, poetry is the place where magic and miracles happen. Words come alive, carry incantations into the imagination and appear on the page miraculously coherent.

I expected to select poetry that moved me from the submissions I read. Instead, I found myself at the intersection of words that brought together shared experiences of the different cultures and worlds of our ancestors.

Even after 50 years of writing and sharing my work, I still feel an enormous obligation to honor my ancestors for their gifts to me and have worked to build and promote community by hosting poetry readings, retreats and reunions.

And even after so many years of writing and sharing my soul work, there is still so much more to give and learn from this art we call poetry. Editing this anthology has been a unique opportunity to honor the gifts of others, an experience that I will always cherish.

Table of Contents

Spanish Conversation by Ethelbert Miller	1
Why is it Greek Omelet and Not Puerto Rican? By Ethelbert Miller	2
Neruda by Ethelbert Miller	3
My Father as Prophet and Provider by Ethelbert Miller	4
Untitled by Ethelbert Miller	5
baby/TALK by Saleem Abdal-Khaaliq	6
Yellow Brick Road by Saleem Abdal-Khaaliq	7
Muse/um by Saleem Abdal-Khaaliq	8
Portrait of the Old South in a New Frame by Saleem Abdal-Khaaliq	10
Caribbean Girl by Sistah Joy Alford	12
Transient by Jane Alberdeston Coralin	15
Toll by Jane Alberdeston Coralin	18
Papi and his Chrysler Cordoba by Jane Alberdeston Coralin	19
Ghost Adventures by Jane Alberdeston Coralin	21
Estate Quieto by Kamilah Valentin Diaz	23
No Sabe Na' by Kamilah Valentin Diaz	25
Thanksgiving by Nick Leininger	26
Equilibrist by Nick Leininger	28

The First Time I Felt Black by Nick Leininger	30
Passing by Nick Leininger	32
Cosquilla by Stephani E. D. McDow	33
ThoughTrain by Stephani E. D. McDow	35
Ode to los Mayate by Manuel Mendez	36
I am Joaquin by Hermond Palmer	38
We Rise, Again by henry 7. reneau, jr.	40
El Dia de los Muertos by henry 7. reneau, jr.	42
Take by Allison Whittenberg	43
Hedy by Allison Whittenberg	44
Lip Service by Allison Whittenberg	45
A by Christine Williams	46
My Why by Jeffrey Banks	47
Racism Poem by Jeffrey Banks	50
Poet's Soup by Maritza Rivera	52
Chips with Ketchup by Maritza Rivera	54

Diaspora Café: D.C.

ETHELBERT MILLER

Spanish Conversation

For Roberto Vargas

in cuba
a dark skin woman asks me
if I'm from angola
i try to explain in the no spanish I know
that i am american

she finds this difficult to believe
at times i do too

ETHELBERT MILLER

Why is it Greek Omelet and Not Puerto Rican

Every morning I
look for you on the menu.
Where are
your eyes and lips,
my side order of thighs?

I'm so hungry for the sauce
of you and the way your
blouse opens
like a flame.

ETHELBERT MILLER

Neruda
For Naomi

Neruda's head is across town.
It's in the garden outside
the OAS building.

I need to go there.
No, I need to find what they
did to the rest of Neruda's body.

Where are Neruda's hands?
Legs? Feet? Did someone believe
Neruda's poems came only from his head?

What does one make love with?
Bring me Neruda's poems!
Ask them to confess.

ETHELBERT MILLER

My Father as Prophet and Provider
For Egberto Miller

He did not speak
often. I only heard
him when he spoke.
My fear of him
rewarded my silence.
His love was a gentle
terror. Out of respect
I was always good.
The fierce light in his
eyes a reminder that
my life would never
succumb to darkness.

ETHELBERT MILLER

Untitled

At the end of the day we learn from our lives and the lives of others
You are either facing a wall or standing against one

SALEEM ABDAL-KHAALIQ

baby/TALK

    if we treated every child like poetry
the history of ourselves would be read
and not forgotten

    if we saw the poetry in our children
we could see their reflection and understand
they are our lasting light

    if we created children like the poet
creates poetry it would be a true act
of love

    if we read the poetry in their eyes
we would not go foolishly
to parenthood

    We would not admonish them vainly
    nor abuse their delicate beginnings
    but we would speak poems to them

    Softly, and watch them grow
    from the essence of our words

SALEEM ABDAL-KHAALIQ

Yellow Brick Road

people of color
with blue collars
& no green card
meet red, white
& blue smiles

head on

in white collars
who use invisible
ink to redline
& blackball

all in the same
    stroke

SALEEM ABDAL-KHAALIQ

Muse/um

in their broke woke/ness
   they deface and topple statues — statuary rape
      often march in crowds for the cause right past

         decayed urban libraries &
         no/net basketball hoops
         once sacred, now scarred
         in parks left for vandals
            smashed windows refuse to reflect
         though terrorized tourists lean from buses
         they've paid to see rather than pay reparations
      their eyes at half-mast

Aunt Jemina & Uncle Ben have left the building
Uncle Remus did too — "Zippy Do-Dah Day"

      Among the gallery of gallows
      a galley of motionless nooses
      mere thought near understanding
      with a negative of Travon Martin
      exposed in black & white digitally — near by

Sister Sadie | Sapphire | Beulah became Beauty Pageant Queens
because they exemplified Hottentot Venus — everybody say Amen!
within this New World there is nothing new…

Buckwheat campaigned for office running on a platform of
Critical Race in Theory anyway, against the have-nots

Where "Ole Back Joe" met up with "Old Black Betty 'in the
 land of cotton
"both of them interrogated Betty Crocker & the King of the
 Wild Frontier
"Bam-A-lam"

  behind portrait glass —
  a splintered magic wand
   (nothing disappears)
  a still-life on imaginary canvas
  no curator can cure because
  it is a relay race — with no baton

 all things have been relegated to the Museum of
  Un-Natural History

Sanford & Son used their GPS to get to A'mos & Andy's crib
 while looking
for John Henry, eating pancakes at Sambo's, despite that
 every one of them
accepted   /Aetna's apology
          Any questions?

SALEEM ABDAL-KHAALIQ

Portrait of the Old South in a New Frame

Our tongues moist in the act
of drawing inner outlines —
shading a portrait in brush whispers

lingering in the nightlight
of oil shadows' thin lacquer
like the quicksand of forgetfulness

when molten desire of mixing colors
not made for blending surfaced
our paint brushes stroked the canvas

strange fruit still lingers in red clay
coffins, crows feet delicately decorate
the faces of the eye-witnesses

silenced by an age of experience
old folks called it:
"… looking not to see …"

clad in floral pastels attempting
to whitewash a charcoal silhouette
into a masterpiece of grey

blood dried acrylic set in a feigned
history by Southern Baptists
& Voodoo Episcopalians

hidden under the Mississippi delta
your canvas dripping oils
onto a Moon/mare of bewilderment

Waxing still before us, to settle on
evening's shade: "In a land of cotton,
old times there are not forgotten
... Look Away!"

JOY ALFORD

Caribbean Girl

The Caribbean girl
Walks down the street
The eyes of all those she meets
Greet her with smiles
For she is their sister
With ancestors from
The Motherland

The Caribbean girl
Walks down the street
She carries baubles, bangles,
Beads of all kinds
They are not trinkets
But her treasures
Memories of the long ago
Memories of where she comes from

The Caribbean girl
Walks down the street
As free as you please
She switches her hips
And walks with the breeze
She is the Caribbean girl!

The Caribbean girl
Shows me the way to freedom
Shows me the way

To release my spirit
To laugh with the sun

And become one with all of creation

The Caribbean girl
Has discovered all the secrets of life
She carries magic in the palm of her hand
She understands and knows the universe
For she has traversed it ten times 'round
It is her playground
The playground of the Caribbean girl

I know the Caribbean girl
I see her dance oh so wild and free
She hears the music and the drum-beat
            the music and the drum-beat
                      the music and the drum-beat

They move her feet in a rhythm
That gently pats the face of Mother Earth
Caressing her, sending her a message of love
Love for the freedom she carries in her soul

Oh, that beat!
So strong in my heart
No matter where I go
I know I shall never part
Never part from the Caribbean girl

My feet dance the beat
That calls and greets the ancestors
Echoing their song of eternity
They rejoice and are proud

It is from them that I garner my strength
From them I have gathered my smile

It is they who have sent me
They that have given me
My smile, my spirit, my dance

It is they who have told me
I am strong
I am eternal
I am the Caribbean girl!

JANE ALBERDESTON CORALIN

Transient

God, whose father was a cane
cutter, was born to be a chief in Otoao, a son-God,
who dreamt of being more, so the boy drew petroglyphs
all along the rocks, and made the village
angry; penniless but joyful, the boy who mornings lay
in morivivi patches and afternoons plucked the skulls
of coconuts, was shipped by his downtrodden father
to spend winters at his uncle's
in Long Island; those icy months
the boy missed his yucayeque,
now what could he do but remember
his father's gruff goodbye, telling him
to learn a trade; here he was, boy and god,
doing the same: hanging with cousins, learning
the English, the get-by and the hustle; this God,
this know-nothing, girl-shy cliché who wrote poems
in the back of a storeroom during his break, was the same
boy-God turned teenager, who dropped his mother's last name,
packed his suitcase, and left that sad island for Harlem,
where the only thing waiting was the moon,
a sign advertising shared rooms. From there,
what could stop him? not even his mama's voice — fading
like a fallen hibiscus bloom; but those watercolors
he couldn't stifle, brushstrokes
in his sleep drew him anyway, migrating, always
coming and going, from one island to another,
from factory floor to pavement, from wharf to plank

to whipping seas, all the tributaries that would lead him
like a fish from a kauhale to a nu to the prefecture
where the young God
would eat, drink and sleep
under the needle of the tebori, until the youth bled
the old ways, bled the lineages, his and all those of Otoao.
When the exploding dusts of two cities slipped
into his inks, he heard another call, grew out his hair,
and flew west to markets where he sold the charcoal
and pastels he mixed, along the way learning a few words
in Arabic; nomads too, God slept among them, their skins
like his, all tins of pigment. They tried to read him, tracing
their fingers against his hieroglyphics, drawn along
the aging tints, but the god knew all those blues
were only corpuscular, and so he yearned for a home,
if not for the one of his births. He opened a small studio
on the edge of Montmartre, but he was shrewder now
and could survive off a love affair with bread.
When love left him and he couldn't sit still,
there was Haight-Ashberry and earth-body work
with Mendieta, then Provincetown where he forgot everything
a god knows. He was grown and tired, and an oncoming
    boy's war
meant he could pretend no more; with his whole name
on his papers and between his lips, God flew back
to Otoao, now Utuado, a city holding his mother under it.
God was back, though you'd think no one knew it, so
    he hitched
a ride to a city named for a saint, to a third-floor walkup
with a twin bed, and a balcony overlooking la calle Luna
and the outline of a fort with its salt militants,
where now the old God leans to see,

where his hand grows shaky,
and the colors aren't as a brilliant as before

Toll

1. In the middle of a hurricane, everybody prays.
2. A devil is the response team; his stratagems cling to whipping seed pods.
3. The screeching clashes with that of ministers, governors and fools.
4. Policemen slip under mudslides; mayors huddle under rooftops thick as lids on sardine cans.
5. Fear cracks floor tiles, reverses mirrors and muffles dreams.
6. A storm counts backward, lingers its foot on hope's neck.
7. A morgue warms. Oxygen tanks are the price of Kobe beef; a saline IV bag? Godiva chocolate.
8. There are no shortcuts to live by, only gas lines and definitions for despair.
9. A war builds on the wharf.
10. Reports that a flight of cheap paper towels lands on the heads of a crowd in Guaynabo City.

> Later, 4600 wet continents wash up on shore.

JANE ALBERDESTON CORALIN

Papi and his Chrysler Cordoba

In his eyes, you could see a salesman's bounty.
Every time Papi looked at his Cordoba
you knew he knew it was not meant to be a family car

but a car for the left lane, with the window down,
with dashboard dice over the gray plush exterior winking back
at the ladies passing, peering in, as if they couldn't get enough

of My Papi, who always waited until it was the hottest hour
of Saturday to wash his Mami. He made it a holy act,
a Sabbath ritual, a cup of overflowing

burgundy, felpa and Turtle wax, so shiny, it reflected back his
face in the sun. This was how he relaxed, never asking for help,
all puffed up, shirt front wet with the whipping hose, suds

in his lashes, as if a rainbow had kissed his eyes. Proud Papi
of the Chrysler Cordoba with the silver and gold siderails,
and the Chrysler insignia bent sideways on the hood

from the time he hit the bicyclist who looked
the other way. It never mattered to him that his back
bent the same, a brace to hold a slipped disc, incurred

falling off an assault tank the way Icarus thudded back
to earth, all melted wax and white feathers, body broken
like a pigeon's heart.

Papi's too was like that, maroon and mystical,
like the surface of a summertime lake, sparkling
with the loosed oil of drowned cars.

JANE ALBERDESTON CORALIN

Ghost Adventures
Washington, D.C.

I haunt the margins of a district, searching songs for love in a city made for clean breaks. All of me wonders if anyone remembers a Fender's bent beats echoing, in the bellies of black buildings, tugging on the last strings of sober in my head. And yet it wasn't only one song, riding the choruses of avenues on the diagonal that called me from within caves and cafes and the dark lining of villanelles and other dress window forms.

{Potomac, remember me. You waited for us after P Street's easy Saturdays, after the last word had left the last mouth before closing. On our swollen lips, the kiss of cakes and tisanes, sestinas teasing us back, our bodies buzzing like mayflies. But it was on your boardwalk I trembled, caught on splinters.}

A city pales in my treads, as I hunt Wisconsin for love beyond reach. Buses meander anxious streets, our crisscross cracks avenues in two. Hands dig for bus fare, $1.10 between one metro stop and romance, and I remember the waxing in the red rows, leaning in a seduction of brick. On a night built on the back wings of waterbugs, we were hopelessly cynical.

Taxis make this city dizzy. Between Logan Circle and the heart of a dying 16th Street vesper you'll find a sweaty hotdog vendor and a waning punch-dream-drunk afternoon of bright boys and paint drums, their ancient go-go.

Because I want, I trouble a ward turn it upside, shake corners loose of metrocards and liquor and tulips, the conceit of dog parks and wainscoting. I watch summer skitter. A phantom in 401s slips beyond the margins of a district's love affair with all things tricked, and I realize it is only me, slinking into alleys riddled with the broken spines of rhyme and other dialogues with god, clinging to the pouty lips of poets and all their schools of solemn.

KAMILAH VALENTIN DIAZ

Estate Quieto

Tus manos no tienen el
derecho a tocarme.
Acariciarme
ni dominarme.

Tus manos lascivas son tuyas
y mi cuerpo es mío.

Que el respeto nunca falte
y si se te olvida
pues salte.

Yo me pertenezco únicamente
y no me dan ganas de compartir
mi templo.

No soy un columpio. Si quieres
entretenimiento
para eso, buscate una montaña
rusa.
Que esta machina está fuera
de servicio.

Chiringa, tampoco soy.
No me podrás enredar en tus
hilos.

Así que no me toques.

Stay Yourself

You have no right
laying your hands on me.
No right to caress me
or attempt to dominate me.

Your lecherous hands are
yours and my body is mine.

May respect never cease
and if you forget
then you're free to leave.

I belong to myself
and have no urge to share my
temple with the likes of you.

I am not a swing-set. If you
want entertainment
go and find a roller coaster to
satiate your need for adrenaline.
This carnival ride is out of
order.

A kite, I am not.
You cannot tangle me up
in your strings.

Do not touch me.

¿Y si pegas?	And if you hit?
Que solo sea en la lotería.	It better only be in the lotto.
Esta propiedad privada tiene dientes.	This private property has teeth.
No me provoques a usarlos.	Don't provoke me into using them.

KAMILAH VALENTIN DIAZ

No Sabe Na'

Por ahí escuche decir
que el racismo no existía.
¿En qué galaxia vivía
que ese embuste se lo creía?

They Don't Know Sh*t

I've heard people say
that racism doesn't exist.
In what galaxy did they live
that they lapped up that lie so
damn quick?

NICK LEININGER

Thanksgiving

I have a series of extended relatives, none of which I really
    relate to
Today we're just people sitting in a room

The table is covered with white food no nutritionist would bring
The room is full of false faiths fortified by hollow hymns
I pretend to know how to sing

Besides blood, I share nothing in their likeness
My father's side makes me ashamed of my whiteness

I haven't seen my black side in several years
They live in a different country

I don't look like them and my mother's mother doesn't
remember me
My father's mother says there's no point in visiting her

Since she won't remember me
I still remember the stories she told to me

Her description of the Caribbean's cascading terrain
The first time she saw snow in the states

Or how even restaurants in the north wouldn't serve black folks
In the past...My father's mother wouldn't want the whites
and the blacks to mix

To this day, she still believes, that dinosaurs didn't exist
What I'm trying to say is...you don't have to ask...who she voted for

I don't want to be the glue that holds people together
I'm tired of constantly having to walk in between
Especially when I'm not allowed to intervene

This Thanksgiving
I'm thankful that tears feel like a distant memory

That people I know, and love remember me
That I reside in a city that feels like home
And that I finally have a place to call my own

NICK LEININGER

Equilibrist

Tightrope walker
You walk so high and so close to the air
If only you fell, such a tough burden to bear
I wonder if you are aware

Not so sure as to what you are after
How you ended up there or what you aspire
To feel your feet, glide up over the street, to feel alive or to feel something higher
Tattered clothes, when was the last time you didn't have holes in your attire?

The path I take is usually on the sidewalk
Lucky for me the voices in my mind are mine and mine alone

I have a roof and bed and a pillow to rest my head
3 meals a day, modern appliances, including a place to refrigerate bread
You lived a few feet from the store next to the store next to my tea shop
The cruelty of the concrete, your life is no better than an animal

I'm sorry you must live this way
I forgive you for calling me a stupid nigger during that summer shift
Stupid is what hurt the most
How did you know I was part Black? Do you know my mom is Jamaican?

Equilibrist
I hope one day you find a home
It's a shame we aren't given the same hand
Although our advantages are by no means equal
I like to think we are equal in spirit

I hope you continue to walk on your rope
The universe is so vast, I'll do my best to hang in the balance

NICK LEININGER

The First Time I Felt Black

I remember the first time I felt black
It wasn't when I looked at family photos of my
blonde-haired self with my black relatives

It wasn't when the employees of the black hair salon
asked me if I was lost while I patiently waited for my mother
to finish getting her hair braided as I carefully read my most
recent edition of the Magic Tree House book series

I didn't feel black when I played with the other black kids
in my neighborhood or when I played with the handful of
black kids that I knew from my private school

I didn't feel black when the white kids asked me
why I loved my nanny so much or when strangers asked
if I was adopted as they suspiciously gazed at my mother

I didn't feel black wearing my dashiki or playing my djembe
at the drum circle - despite my ability to exhibit a strange and
uncommon affinity for West African polyrhythms

I didn't feel black at the BBQ clearly looking out of race
and out of place

I was in 9th grade on the bus ride home the first time I felt black

A kid I thought was my friend went on a long rant about "n*ggers"

I took a look around and realized I was the only black person on this bus

This was the first time I used violence outside of self defense I used my hands instead of my voice, I felt like I didn't have a choice

His words felt like an attack, this was the first time I felt black

NICK LEININGER

Passing

They think that I'm white
The truth is that I am white
But I'm also black

STEPHANI E. D. MCDOW

Cosquilla

you provided for me make-believe-come-real
    fairy tales tangible and new

you added texture to my paintings
    grains of heaven engulfed in color and hue

linear needs met wavy dreams and formed you

curious about your beginnings after my acceptance of now
    I believed,
let go and inhaled the sweetness of your song
    (knew then that one's breath tastes like the Caribbean fruit
    that intoxicates and kneads my independence into your
      silly putty)

ooh and so warm and new
    I'd dreamed of one day meeting then
    having you

only to wake and find
    never true
    never mine
    never more for real

or as real as my heart made you
    I feel

determining farce from evident is beneath my ill-acceptable
   abilities today
      and it is in these that, sadly, my uncertainties now lay

when ... I just want to hear it again

and
be who I've dreamed of me.

STEPHANI E. D. MCDOW

ThoughTrain

An empty kiss won't suffice
   though considered and daunted upon
   rendering a finality of pointlessness and
void.

Absolution of touches missed
   radiate louder than a steel chisel against a tin drum
   cracking me down the center and
shaking truth to defeat.

Depressing titles show minimalist interest in
   heartfelt understanding, in
   other folk shoe-wearing, in
simply, silently listening.

Not asking to be fixed is
   seemingly overlooked and
   friends break out the tools and lumber anyway
instead of just letting.

It's only the beginning of
   the intermission. Get some Goobers
   Powder your noses.
Life will resume... shortly...

MANUEL MENDEZ

Ode to los Mayate

I realized it early (desde niño)
I realized it after our conversation when you told me,
¡No sos negro!
Ellos son mayate
Tú hablas español.
Cuando hablabas de mi
y pensaste que no te entendía
Cuando quería
jugar, bailar, o tu amistad
y me miraste como un salvaje
O cuando miraste a mi cabello y mi nariz
y me dijiste
"Vos es un mayate"
Y cuando miraba a Univisión gritaste
"ese negro si es feo!"
y cuando me escupiste
y me llamaste perro
allí comprendí mi negritud
y reconocí lo mayate que soy

MANUEL MENDEZ

Ode to los Mayate

translation by Maritza Rivera

I realized it early (from childhood)
I realized it after our conversation when you told me,
You are not Black!
They are mayate
You speak Spanish.
When you talked about me
 and thought I didn't understand you
When I wanted
 to play, dance or your friendship
 you looked at me like I was a savage
 Or when you looked at my hair and my nose
 and told me
"You are a mayate"
And when you watched Univision and yelled
"that black one sure is ugly!"
 and when you spit at me
 and called me a dog
 that's when I understood my blackness
 and recognized the mayate that I am.

HERMOND PALMER

I am Joaquin

I ...
I am Joaquin
the everyman

I am a part of you
just as you
are a part of me

Your history
is my history

Your future
my future

Because we are in this
together

Yo Soy
Joaquin

Su idioma
es mi idioma

Su gente
es mi gente
su familia, mi familia

I see in you
the many layers
textures and complexities
the myriad of possibilities and promise
that make up my life

We
are Joaquin
and what we are is
different, but the same
and together
that makes us
beautiful.

henry 7. reneau, jr

We Rise, Again.

inspired by the words of Luis Antonio Pichardo, Founder &
Executive Director of DSTL Arts

In this time of pandemic   protest & rebellion   many
have declared they believe
in fighting for Social Justice &   Equity for all. But many
have not reflected a past history
of doing precisely that. Have not
historically acknowledged our Diaspora.

As a boy   as a teen   & as a Black man
I have been profiled.
I have been followed.
I have been stopped
for no reason & handcuffed
because I *fit the description.*
I have been harassed & detained   & manhandled by police.

I don't believe all cops are racist thugs. Some
really want to protect & serve. Think
of trying to empty a vast ocean of racism
brutality & murder   with a teaspoon. Or   if one cop is a racist
murdering thug
& ten thousand cops standby & do nothing
then ten thousand &
one cops are racist murdering thugs. Period.

To do nothing
is just as bad as doing the wrong something. As bad as
the white supremacists' fear
of Black bodies. As bad as stereotyped
a thug life gang validated tattoo. A fear of me &
mine. I cannot forget that I am not equal   that we
are not equal.

But I have learned to live with that damaging fact
because
our voices have immense worth
accumulated through centuries of being
intoned against.

We are not a footnote. Are not a trend.
We are as many as you can think of   plus one more.

I will no longer lightly walk behind
a one of you who fear me:
*   Be afraid.*

  Note: the italicized text is by June Jordan from
    I Must Become a Menace to My Enemies.

henry 7. reneau, jr

El Dia de los Muertos

*Explosions ripped through
a fireworks market north
of Mexico City on Tuesday,
killing at least 35 people.*
    –December 20, 2016

Smoke billows
la muerte / tragedy-blackened
clouds because
sometimes /

God doesn't care /
about the body count //   For
whom / the bells toll /   or
collateral damage //

Si dios quiere, His
capriciousness of / chaos claws
& blur of hooked beak //   Of fire &
smoke / & the after-ash

of grief /   in God's absentia //

ALLISON WHITTENBERG

Take

The truth from
The story to create
The myth that becomes
The history that is taken as
The truth
that we die for.

ALLISON WHITTENBERG

Hedy

beauty,
the curse
that coursed
through her

aggressively

moveover, how dare
she have a brain
under
such a face

all this was said to be so ... unfortunate

pretty and smart?
unfortunate?

that's a joke — right?

ALLISON WHITTENBERG

Lip Service

... that hollywood star
is so woke
the only black person
she has on her instagram
is George Floyd.

CHRISTINE WILLIAMS

A

I love the way you open your mouth and use your tongue…
   to make sounds
Your accent is like music to my ears.

Your body is my favorite chocolate.
I want to taste it all the time.

Your work ethic and ambition turns me on.
It is almost as sexy as your face.

The way you pay attention to me makes me feel so loved
   and respected.
I love when you do that shit!

I also love when you go slow for me.

I love you.
Te Quiero.
Je vous aime.
Mwen renmen ou.

JEFFREY BANKS

My Why

As I spend half of the first week of school in court I realize
my why

Christmas day 2018 on the Metro I was assaulted
most people couldn't care any less I was insulted
but instead of elementary the boy was 19
I can't say what were the missteps if any
in his upbringing but here's the part I can play

Oftentimes, many will mistake strength for weakness,
my meekness shows caring at all times the divine
will give me the unction to strive, to be the conjunction
wherever there's a disconnect my effect
I may never know but the rare glow I get
when I know I affect a young person positively

Kids encountered me when they were the height
of my knee and come back to me fifteen years later
in a Walmart saying, "Mr. Banks!"
they just wanted to thank me for the brief time I
was their educator and the reward of someone
remembering me means we were both the greater for it

My why, for young men Black and Brown,
adolescent boys don't realize how much society
frowns on males, their hue, not knowing what to do do,
the things they do for attention are sometimes
unmentionable, the placement in special ed is

sometimes justified but in any placement one can
learn the desire to 'live your best life' has to burn
so in hopes of not going back and forth
as in the song building the resilience to achieve
that will be life-long and that is my why

I am that guy who was in special ed back in pre-K
I didn't 'have it made' but I 'became the magnificent'
when my Mama prayed and to this day she advocates
fought for me to get the best, to ignite my greatness
my special needs to exceeding teacher's expectations
I'm a talented and gifted creation
my mother advocated for my mind to be stimulated

Many young people my hue don't see a man
in the classroom
no struggle no progress
so as they know struggle they will know progress
I'll be their Frederick Douglass
abolishing excuses and speaking to their greatness
so they know someone believes they can achieve
and someone cares even years later I'm thankful
they're aware when I see students, now parents,
fighting the good fight, remember me as I
guard their building when they sleep at night
my why.

When former students are now service providers
whether retwisting my locs or in my Lyft ride
they're striving for higher it's always clear
Mr. Banks is here for them and is their cheerleader
no matter what I want them to win
my reason 'why' is they have it within and to win

doesn't have to be at another's expense
I don't want any young person to catch an offense
this life has taught me never to give up
and on any young person I'll never give up

My struggles yield progress
I'll help them through struggles so they'll
get to progress
the spit that was put on me the good book said
made a blind man see so my why I know
for some young person to learn I am that guy!

JEFFREY BANKS

Racism Poem

Racism is as American as red, white and blue,
Tried and true ever since I could tie my shoe
I've had to fight for my seat at the table
My God was able to have ella advocate
So special ed was not my fate
K-12 she knew full well Jeffrey was gifted
So I was lifted past White kids in New Milford
Who thought my skin was brown I did not wash
And I looked like 'burnt popcorn'
You'd think adults knew better in the eighties
But a lady known as my babysitter said a teacher
Referred to her and her Latina friend as 'Spic and Spook'
Do you think the move from Connecticut to Florida gets better?
Of course there are better efforts to #HashTagAHomey
Because the confederate flag raises high on I-75
To this day

In the ninth grade a fellow kid thought it was alright to play
Grabbing an Asian girl and when I told him to stop this is what
Hurled from his mouth: fat a** N****R

That's what he said before he flew across the room
When they tried to suspend me my receipts rang true
Saving me an getting him in trouble it's a shame
I have to do double to get only half the respect only to
Protect my neck classmates called me 'slave' and expected
Me to behave I'm all about 'unity in the community' but
When a cop asked a White friend if I was causing trouble in

A bowling alley when we were conversing in peace the '8'
For new beginnings in NOT a release but the pool ball
Identified as the color of my skin no one gives a flip
How much someone offends me in a traffic stop or
The workplace my work history is probably a disgrace
Two graduate degrees and my earning potential is a dearth
White principal treated me as the scum of the the earth
Bit by a child and and hospitalized he called me
the N word a dozen times and to my surprise my response
Was to tell the child, "my name is Mr. Banks' and the
Way I was thanked at the end of the year was a 'RIF'
That turned into a pink slip and the appeal turned into
Sealed files yet we're not supposed to act vile and be
Senile to perpetual abuse after being opporessed for
So long you get used to being treated as 'a poor excuse for
A man' deserving to be pulled over at all of these planned
'Driving while Black' traffic stops few warrant a ticket
But when it brings a cop to evict you from your car
And it goes to get towed when you finally get to court
Just then you're NOW told that it's found your car
Was wrongly impounded but now nothing can be done
The game police play just for fun is at a Black Man's expense
Being locked up for a broken taillight and an unpaid ticket
Leading to a suspended license doesn't make sense
But two cops high five when I arrived in the back of a
Police cruiser for this I'm beyond pissed but Ella taught
Her boys "cops shoots first and ask questions later"
I'm used to the abuse from the ugly hater called racism
That has me on fire and so many try to extinguish this man
So educated yet so feared because he's so big so Black
Seen as a threat and if killed america will believe that

MARITZA RIVERA

Poet's Soup

The proof of a savory soup
is in a well seasoned broth
warming us from the inside out
always thicker and tastier the next day.

It starts with a drizzle of olive oil
fresh from Palermo, chopped garlic,
julienned green peppers and Spanish
onions sautéed in salty tears.

There are no secret ingredients
in grandmother's hearty recipe
just foreign lands and people who
emigrated with her so long ago.

Exotic flavors play on our tongues
like kids do at the park.

Rustic staples
find their home
in new cultures:

Russet potatoes, Jasmine rice, Ramen noodles,
beans sometimes refried, plantains cooked green or ripe.

The sear of meat-fish-poultry curls in the air
dances up our nose and rings in our ear
like Nana's voice calling us for supper.

Sometimes, something as simple as soup
is enough to gather us at a common table
of generations: families, friends and even foes
to slurp, laugh and belch with satisfaction.

Everyone gathered here also brings
something special to the table.

Communities can be like that too
where our children grow
play and learn together

creating memories from the recipes
we've handed down to them with love
and so much more.

MARITZA RIVERA

Chips with Ketchup

In 1965, potatoes were thinly sliced,
deep fried and served in cone shaped
dixie cups with ketchup.

After school let out from St. Cecilia's
Catholic School in Manhattan, a parade of
crimson and white uniforms marched to
the 5 and dime store on the corner of
106th and 3rd.

We'd scatter like nuns in the casino scene of
Sister Act and converge at the lunch
counter for freshly fried chips with ketchup.

This was our special treat at a time when
lunch counters elsewhere were scenes of
unrest, violence and hatred in southern parts
of the country we didn't know existed.

Civil rights weren't an issue for
12-year-old Hispanic, Black, Italian
and Irish school girls, who shared
religion, education and cones of
chips with ketchup on the Upper
East Side of New York City in 1965.

At that time in our young girls' lives
nothing else seemed more important
than chips with ketchup.

Times are much different for
12-year-old girls nowadays.

Appendix of Contributor Bios

SALEEM ABDAL-KHAALIQ was born and raised in Massachusetts and has spent many years in California. His written works are essentially experimental and often meet at the nexus of conscience and visceral utterance. He is the author of Mind Sand – Selected Poems by Saleem Abdal-Khaaliq. The book of poems addresses our shifting thoughts, like sand that leave trail impressions never before imagined. Saleem's work has appeared in Chronogram Magazine and several anthologies including River Crossings: Voices of the Diaspora and a literary journal, Signifyin' Harlem: The Next Generation. He attended Howard University in Washington, D.C.

J. JOY "SISTAH JOY" ALFORD is the inaugural Poet Laureate of Prince George's County, Maryland. She is the author of 3 books of poetry: Lord I'm Dancin' As Fast As I Can, From Pain to Empowerment - The Fabric of My Being, and This Garden Called Life. She received the 2002 Poet Laureate Special Award from the DC Commission on the Arts and Humanities for her outstanding contributions to the art of poetry in her native Washington, DC. She has served as President of the Ebenezer Poetry Ministry since 2003 and was named Poet Laureate of Ebenezer AME Church in 2016. She produces and hosts the award-winning TV show, "Sojourn with Words," which airs on CTV in Prince George's County and Montgomery County, MD, and can now be viewed globally through its virtual format on YouTube and Zoom. Sistah Joy is an activist poet who founded Collective Voices, a poetry ensemble whose members present messages of social consciousness, inspiration, and empowerment. She has performed throughout the U.S. and in the U.K.

JEFFREY BANKS is poetically known as "Big Homey." His credits include: ESSENCE Magazine, Sirius/XM Satellite Radio, Radio-One Inc., the CBS Early Show, BLACK ENTERPRISE Magazine, performing nationwide, international broadcasts, multiple grant awards and publications through DC Public Libraries, the National Association for Poetry Therapy, Paris Lit Up, and Day Eight.

JANE ALBERDESTON CORALIN lived in Washington DC between 1994 and 2002. Washington DC was where lived the word, from being a virgin at The Fifteen Minutes Club on 15th Street, to waiting to get on the list upstairs at It's Your Mug on P, to Mount Pleasant where she performed at the Gala Hispanic Theater, to spending a summer reading under the stars in Rock Creek Park. Like all children, these were her formative years, where she played and fell and got back up to do it all over again. That beloved city is the place where Jane first called herself poet. A proud alumna of the DC writers community, Cave Canem, and Binghamton University (NY), Jane returned to the island of her birth in 2008, where she teaches literature and creative writing at the University of Puerto Rico in Arecibo. She continues to work on her poetry, recently completed a collection of poems, and is working on a novel, due to be released in 2023.

KAMILAH MERCEDES VALENTÍN DÍAZ is a Boricua with Indigenous, African, and Spanish ancestry, born in Puerto Rico, and living in the diaspora in the United States. As a child she was always interested in the written word and oftentimes found herself escaping to fantastical worlds. She would craft and share wild stories for anyone who would listen. As she grew, she began writing randomly with unfinished works scattered about in multiple journals. It wasn't until 2021 that she realized her writings weren't random; they were poetry. Kamilah now identifies as a self-proclaimed poetisa, and is in the process of writing her first poetry collection for publication with Alegria Publishing. Morivivi: To have Died, yet Lived, in confessional style poetry, will cover her mental health journey, themes of identity and womanhood, and her beloved Puerto Rico. If you are interested in following Kamilah on her journey towards publication and other adventures she can be found on Instagram through the handle @kams_conchispas.

NICK LEININGER is a DC poet originally from West Chester, Pennsylvania. Nick graduated from American University in 2017 with a bachelor's degree in Public Relations and Strategic Communications. During his days as a student, Nick had his poem "The Sin of Omission" published in the 2017 edition of Bleakhouse Publishing's Tacenda magazine. Nick also has poems featured in BourgeonOnline, and his poem "Broken" is featured in the 2021 Day Eight poetry anthology, The Great World of Days. Nick has been using poetry as a tool of self-reflection throughout the 2020-2021 COVID19 pandemic.

STEPHANI E. D. MCDOW is a poet and writer who has been published in Raven Chronicles Press' Take a Stand: Art Against Hate Anthology, Still Point Arts Quarterly, Genre: Urban Arts No. 7, Femme Literati: Mixtape Anthology, and armarolla. Formerly a contributing author at Woman Around Town and freelance writer/editor, Stephani's work has been praised by award-winning editor, writer and journalist, Susan L. Taylor; and award-winning author and editor, Charlene Giannetti. Stephani is a nonprofit and professional development consultant, speaker, trainer and social justice advocate. A native D.C. Washingtonian, she currently resides in Maryland and is working on completing her first novel.

MANUEL MENDEZ, Chair for the DC AfroLatino Caucus, is originally from the Dominican Republic and moved to Washington, D.C. at the age of nine. After graduating from Bell Multicultural High School, Mr. Mendez received his bachelor's degree in African Studies and Communication at Antioch College in Yellow Springs, Ohio. Fortunate to have a host of mentors in his adolescence, Mr. Mendez's passion for supporting positive youth development and the issues that plague the people of the African Diaspora are ever apparent themes in his pursuit of progressive change in his community. A constant in the Columbia Heights neighborhood, Mr. Mendez's dedicated support has allowed him to forge long-term meaningful relationships with members of the community. Currently as the chair of the DC AfroLatino Caucus, Mr. Mendez's goal is to unite "black and brown" people of the Washington metropolitan area.

E. ETHELBERT MILLER is a literary activist and author of two memoirs and several poetry collections. He hosts the WPFW morning radio show On the Margin with E. Ethelbert Miller and hosts and produces The Scholars on UDC-TV which received a 2020 Telly Award. Miller has conducted poetry workshops for incarcerated individuals at the Montgomery County Correctional Facility (MCCF) in Boyds, Maryland. Most recently, he was given a grant from the D.C. Commission on the Arts and Humanities and a congressional award from Congressman Jamie Raskin in recognition of his literary activism. Miller's latest book is When Your Wife Has Tommy John Surgery and Other Baseball Stories (City Point Press, 2021).

HERMOND PALMER has performed his poetry in Harlem, Philadelphia, Washington DC, Atlanta and the Black Arts Festival. He has been a featured poet of the Moonstone Arts Center and on The Writer's Haven with V. Helene. He has written several books of poetry including Echoes from the Quiet that I Keep, Open Mic Words to Fill the Light in You, What the Ancestors Told Me and I Decided to Listen, and a forthcoming novel of fiction entitled Road Kings.

henry 7. reneau, jr. writes words of conflagration to awaken the world ablaze, an inferno of free verse illuminated by his affinity for disobedience—is the spontaneous combustion that blazes from his heart, phoenix-fluxed red & gold, like a discharged bullet that commits a felony every day, exploding through change is gonna come to implement the fire next time. He is the author of the poetry collection, freedomland blues (Transcendent Zero Press) and the e-chapbook, physiography of the fittest (Kind of a Hurricane Press), now available from their respective publishers. Additionally, his collection, A Non-Violent Suicide Poem [or, The Saga of The Exit Wound], was a finalist for the 2022 Digging Press Chapbook Series. His work is published in Superstition Review, TriQuarterly, Prairie Schooner, Zone 3; Poets Reading the News and Rigorous. His work has also been nominated multiple times for the Pushcart Prize and Best of the Net.

MARITZA RIVERA is a Puerto Rican poet and Army veteran who has lived in Rockville, MD since 1994. She has been writing poetry for over fifty years; is the creator of a short form of poetry called Blackjack and is the publisher of Casa Mariposa Press. Maritza is the author of About You; A Mother's War, written during her son's two tours in Iraq; Baker's Dozen; Twenty-One: Blackjack Poems and creator of the Blackjack Poetry Playing Cards. Her work appears in literary magazines, anthologies and online publications and in the public arts project, Meet Me at the Triangle in Wheaton, MD. In 2011, Maritza began hosting the annual Mariposa Poetry Retreat, "where the magic of poetry happens", which takes place in Puerto Rico in 2022.

ALLISON WHITTENBERG is an award-winning poet, short story writer, playwright, and novelist. Her novels are Sweet Thang, Hollywood and Maine, Life is Fine, Tutored (Random House 2006, 2008, 2009, and 2010). Her work has appeared in Flying Island, Feminist Studies, Inconclast, and The Ekphrastic Review. She is author of the full-length short story collection, Carnival of Reality (Loyola University Press, 2022). Whittenberg is a three-time Pushcart Prize nominee.

CHRISTINE WILLIAMS is a Maryland poet and artist. She writes poems based on life experiences. When it comes to her art, her favorite medium to work with is yarn on canvas. She appreciates patterns and making various shapes by mixing colors of yarn and making a work of art. However, she likes to express herself through various ways. Christine is as unique and bold as the art she creates.

Index of Contributors and Poem Titles

A by Christine Williams	46
Abdal-Khaaliq, Saleem	6–10
Alford, Sistah Joy	12
baby/TALK by Saleem Abdal-Khaaliq	6
Banks, Jeffrey	47–50
Caribbean Girl by Sistah Joy Alford	12
Chips with Ketchup by Maritza Rivera	54
Coralin, Jane Alberdeston	15–21
Cosquilla by Stephani E. D. McDow	33
Diaz, Kamilah Valentin	23–25
El Dia de los Muertos by henry 7. reneau, jr.	42
Equilibrist by Nick Leininger	28
Estate Quieto by Kamilah Valentin Diaz	23
Ghost Adventures by Jane Alberdeston Coralin	21
Hedy by Allison Whittenberg	44
I am Joaquin by Hermond Palmer	38
Leininger, Nick	26–32
Lip Service by Allison Whittenberg	45
McDow, Stephani E. D.	33–35
Miller, Ethelbert	1–5
Mendez, Manuel	36
Muse/um by Saleem Abdal-Khaaliq	8

My Father as Prophet and Provider by Ethelbert Miller	4
My Why by Jeffrey Banks	47
Neruda by Ethelbert Miller	3
No Sabe Na' by Kamilah Valentin Diaz	25
Ode to los Mayate by Manuel Mendez	36
Palmer, Hermond	38
Papi and his Chrysler Cordoba by Jane Alberdeston Coralin	19
Passing by Nick Leininger	32
Poet's Soup by Maritza Rivera	52
Portrait of the Old South in a New Frame by Saleem Abdal-Khaaliq	10
Racism Poem by Jeffrey Banks	50
reneau jr., henry 7.	40–42
Rivera, Maritza	52–54
Spanish Conversation by Ethelbert Miller	1
Take by Allison Whittenberg	43
Thanksgiving by Nick Leininger	26
The First Time I Felt Black by Nick Leininger	30
ThoughTrain by Stephani E. D. McDow	35
Toll by Jane Alberdeston Coralin	18
Transient by Jane Alberdeston Coralin	15

Untitled by Ethelbert Miller	5
We Rise, Again by henry 7. reneau, jr.	40
Whittenberg, Alison	43–45
Why is it Greek Omelet and Not Puerto Rican? by Ethelbert Miller	2
Williams, Christine	46
Yellow Brick Road by Saleem Abdal-Khaaliq	7

ABOUT DAY EIGHT

Day Eight's vision is to be part of the healing of the world through the arts, and our mission is to empower individuals and communities to participate in the arts through the production, publication, and promotion of creative projects.

Day Eight's programming includes an online magazine, poetry events, live arts programming, book publishing, arts journalism, and education programs for children and youth.

Example 2021 projects include:

The DC Arts Writing Fellowship was created to support early career arts writers. The project is conducted in partnership with local news outlets including Tagg Magazine and The DC Line. An annual conference brings together leaders in the field of arts journalism.

The DC Poet Project is a poetry reading series and open-to-all poetry competition
that supports the professional practice of poetry. The 2020 instance of the DC Poet Project was produced through support from the Wells Fargo Community Foundation and the National Endowment for the Arts.

Day Eight's projects in local art history included an online archive dedicated to DC's first artist cooperative gallery, the Jefferson Place Gallery.

All of Day Eight's projects are made possible by the support of volunteers and individual donors, including the Board of Directors. To learn more about the organization please visit www.DayEight.org.